W9-CHI-401

By William Goyen

A BOOK OF
JESUS

A BOOK OF
JESUS

William Goyen

DOUBLEDAY & COMPANY, INC.

GARDEN CITY, NEW YORK

1973

UNITY SCHOOL LIBRARY

DISCARD

Lee's Summit, Missouri 64063

ISBN: 0-385-05979-5
Library of Congress Catalog Card Number 72–84915
Copyright © 1973 by William Goyen
All Rights Reserved
PRINTED IN THE UNITED STATES OF AMERICA
FIRST EDITION

This little book is for
Michael, son
and for his mother, Doris
and his grandmother, Ann

and remembering with love
the houses of
Martha and Jim
and
Bruce and Art

Contents

Author's Note

I have drawn the information for this little book from the four Gospels of the New Testament, Matthew, Mark, Luke, and John, but I have followed mainly the sequence and arrangement of events as recorded by Mark. All quotations are from the King James Version, and sometimes the Scriptures are paraphrased.

I have wanted to uncover the strange, remarkable, and sometimes hidden life of this man, as he walked through humanity from his baptism to his crucifixion, primarily for those who do not know it or who know it dimly. For those who know this life, it is always new.

My intention has not been to interpret or analyze. The material preaches itself. I have hoped, simply, to try to tell again the story of the man, his world, his times, the people around him.

W.G.

I

A Brief Life of Jesus

THE world as it was then was the world that has always been: made worse by man and needing change. The rich and the powerful politicians were overtaxing and cheating the poor. Some people had a lot and many had little. Freedom and abundance belonged to the same men. There was want and suffering and injustice. The religious laws were irrelevant, but because these laws were of an ancient tradition they were presumed to be right. To violate them was criminal, to question them was blasphemous. Religious faith was cold obeyance of the law, which was an old strict set of rules. The graveness and pretentiousness of religious authorities and holy men were enough to turn men into heathens and revolutionaries. Some change was imperative. The time had come, the time was "fulfilled." It was around A.D. 28 or 29, in a region along the Mediterranean called Palestine, which was occupied by the Romans under Caesar.

A young man named John came out of the wilderness beyond the Dead Sea like lightning. His passion had the threat of violence under it. His mouth opened and his mighty voice bellowed out against his generation; he called them vipers. He warned that the ax was going to strike at the very root of what was corrupt and it would be cut down like bad fruit trees and cast into the fire. There must be a change in every man. Water would give freshness to the stale spirits of men and women. People flocked to him and listened in a spell. The River Jordan was alive with people being baptized in it by John the Baptist.

It was the time for another young man (he, too, was around thirty). He rose and left his home and appeared before John at the river. This man, named Jesus, had been living in the small town of Nazareth, in Galilee, working as a carpenter.

Jesus came to John and said, "Baptize me." "But I'm not worthy to tie the laces of your shoes," John answered. "Baptize me," said Jesus. And so began the swift brief action of the man who divided the history of the world.

When he came up from beneath the water "straightaway," thrust as if from a womb, his feeling was just that, of being reborn out of the depths and darkness. In baptism he saw a new way and was given direction for a new life. He was refreshed, reformed, "cleansed."

A new force was entering the world. A revolution was beginning. A new brotherhood, a new kind of community was being born, here by the river. What made men bitter, empty, hopeless, what ate at the spirit, what soured the soul, would be thrown over. Young men would gather and follow a new leader. Restless in their towns, lost in knowing what to do with their lives in a world that offered them no door, they would "turn around," "renovate." They would find their dignity and they would get it for others. Such a brotherhood began with the coming together of John the Baptist and Jesus: and Jesus took it forward.

BUT first he had to be alone. Jesus went off into the wilderness. He spent forty days alone, struggling with tremendous temptation. His thoughts had to do with whether he was worthy and capable of giving his life utterly to other men, and whether the wrong kind of "success" would defeat him. Could he do it? Self-doubt, sometimes called Satan, took hold of him in the wilderness. After all, he did have a body; he was a man; he did have desires, needs, hungers, vulnerabilities. He could groan and sigh and weep and anger and hurt. Would he be able, finally, to give up the world that he would come to love so much and that would hurt him so? But when he knew that he could do what he had to do, he came back out of the wilderness, ready.

He then moved on, swiftly, under the power of the full new Spirit in him.

BUT when he came back to John's place by the river he was told that John had been seized by the king, Herod, and thrown into prison. Herod had married his brother's wife and John had denounced the marriage as adulterous. Herod had feared the power of this young rebel anyway, for John was becoming too powerful and his influence too widespread: he was inflaming young followers from towns and cities and sending them out to work, secretly or openly, against power and injustice.

This was a serious turn of events and it gave a new urgency to the work Jesus had to do. Now he must waste no time in taking over John's work for God's sake and for John's sake, for the wild, hot-blooded John who had put him under the living water and changed the course of his life. His enemies were John's enemies and his work was among these people and those they abused and neglected. If there was a feeling of vengeance in Jesus, it was a holy vengeance that moved him to set people free from enslavement and persecution. Jesus therefore knew at the outset of his brief earthly career that he was going to be involved in a political situation as well as a social and spiritual one. If he spoke out against certain institutions and rules and laws he was in danger of being considered a subversive, a spy, an enemy of government. People would soon try to force him to be a political and revolutionary Messiah or a member of the royal line of David. They would try to force upon him the title of "King," in the wrong sense.

This is the kind of situation then that Jesus was entering when he headed for Galilee with his new vision, hardened and bitterly tempered by his time alone in the wilderness and with his new words, his gift of tongue. He headed at once for Galilee, speaking and telling, along the road. Jesus was a man of the road. He walked and talked. And although he talked from boats on the lake, on the shore, on mountains, in deserts, and in people's houses, he was more often on the road moving in the midst of people thronging around him. What was he saying? The time is *now*, he was saying, right here at hand. He meant the time for change, first in every man's own being, and second in the world he lived in. The Kingdom of God is here where we all are, right here in this place and in us, in each of us, a personal possession, a beautiful and joyous thing. Turn to me, come to me, follow me —I will show you how simple it is to love and to forgive and to have faith—which is the definition of the "Kingdom of God." "Come into this new Kingdom." This is what the walking Jesus was saying. It was good, fresh news, not gloomy with threats of hellfire and punishment, attendant with fear and self-abasement. It was joy! It was freedom! It was love! No law, no complicated checklist of acceptable and unacceptable do's and don'ts. These words were Jesus' walking words, and in them lay the simple definition of what he meant by the new "Kingdom," by the "Way." People had never before heard such things. They threw down what they were doing and went right with him.

This young, new teacher on the road toward Galilee, coming from the river and his baptism, fired by the imprisonment of his beloved brother John, poured out love from a bottomless pitcher. As he passed along the lake (which was called the Sea of Galilee), he saw two brothers named Simon and Andrew, casting fishing nets. He asked them to join him. They came to him without a question. A little farther along Jesus saw two more brothers, James and John, working with their father in his fishing boat. Jesus invited them to come along.

These five young men were beginning a new society. To realize how astonishing the ideas of Jesus were, you have to understand that nobody had ever said such things before and in such simplicity and with such glowing love and with such a magical, personal presence. Jesus' words were already causing a sensation along the road. From this time on he would be surrounded by multitudes coming upon him from the towns and villages. No wonder rulers would be afraid of him! He drew the poor and the sick and the dispirited to him. These had always been taught of a cold, imperial and impersonal God, hidden from human beings by ritual and edict and code—a programmed God. Jesus was saying I've got a new way: in your heart; love; giving; forgiving. You don't have to receive God's news through the straining mind of decrepit seminarians, boring theologians, pretentious Bible scholars, and dull archaeological diggers. God is new and fresh for each of us—the first time for each. He comes filling you with light and warmth. You take him as you can. You are your own law. Look in your own heart and you will know what to do. I will help you be free. You are somebody and you are loved. The "Kingdom of God" is not a vague, ethereal, unattainable realm. The Kingdom is within *you*. Everybody carries it within *himself*.

There was an uproar!

They went into the town of Capernaum, a lakeside town that was to become one of the principal homes-on-the-road for Jesus. On the Sabbath Jesus went into the local church and spoke and talked. The congregation was shocked by what he was

12

saying, because it was contrary to what the other teachers had been saying. He was also quite critical, and the manner in which he talked was informal and beloved. The others, whom the congregation were used to—the scribes, the elders, the Pharisees—were formal, removed, spoke long, gabby prayers; were solemn and uttered warnings.

Who is this man? they asked. What is his authority? What new doctrine is this? One man had reacted so violently to Jesus' words that he went into a rage and screamed out "Who do you think you are, Jesus from Nazareth, coming in here and acting like the Holy One of God?" But Jesus was able to quiet him by his gentleness, and when the man's rage had left him and he was serene, the people remarked that Jesus had miraculously removed the man's "unclean spirit" from him and they saw that he could heal the mad and the possessed, the unclean of mind and spirit.

News of the healing spread like wildfire and blazed through the town. In fact, when Jesus left the church and went to Simon's house there in Capernaum to have some supper with Simon and his wife and family, a crowd gathered at the door bringing the sick and those "possessed with devils" like the enraged man in church. It seemed the whole town was there in Simon's door yard. Jesus actually had to flee from Simon's house early the next morning to a hiding place beyond the town so as to avoid the mobs.

Along with his four friends, Simon (renamed Peter, meaning "The Rock"), Andrew, James, and John, he moved on to other towns in the territory so that Jesus could preach and help elsewhere. It seemed, however, that people were so much in need of physical help that they sought his consolation and healing power for their afflictions more often than they wanted to hear his new ideas. He had gained an immediate reputation and overnight notoriety for his startling acts of healing. To see a cripple lift himself to his feet and dance with joy astonished people, and to watch a deaf woman yell out "I hear! I hear!"—for Jesus had said to her "Open up!"—was a crowd-drawing spectacle. The roads were filled with people carrying their sick in their arms, on their backs and on cots. Curing and healing the afflicted—people with defects, such as "palsy," withered limbs—meant for Jesus making them whole again. He wanted people clean and whole, "altogether," as we would say. He wanted a unity of the physical being as well as of the spiritual being, and he set great stock in mending fragments, putting together what was broken, and so bringing back physical dignity and fullness to the individual.

A glimpse into the human insights of this man: He knew that to do something against oneself is to *break up* oneself, away from his center. Suffering follows when we divide ourselves and lose our oneness, our self-union, is what he was saying. What we seek is the solid, strong, centered self, to be of "single purpose," "whole-hearted." Otherwise we are confused, our actions are exaggerated or impotent, "one-sided," "half-hearted," "of two minds." Since the "Kingdom of God" is within each man, he who degrades himself (not according to "Law" but *in his own eyes*—for clearly "Law" cannot remove the inner bondages of men) degrades the Kingdom within him, disorganizes, adulterates, "sins against" his inner Kingdom. Over and over again he uses the words "mend," "bind up." The people of his time were very much like the people of our time. They were living in a world that was without a center and falling into pieces. They were "dismembered." Jesus wanted to heal up this society around him by *reforming* it, and he wanted to restore to all human beings the sense of membership, fellowship, brotherhood, kingdom. All these words were Jesus' words and they had a literal meaning, a real application to the world as it was right then, as well as embodying his vision of humanity.

Already the authorities had their eye on him. Who was this man? What would he do next? He was performing wonders and he was challenging their rules and laws. Who knew what kind of mass mania he might incite with his power over enormous gatherings. How to manage this man? Jesus was already aware of the law's eye on him. He was never an advertiser of himself or a showoff. It was not only a part of his humility but an act of shrewdness and circumspection when he "cleansed" a leper and told him to go quietly away, be glad he was clean, try to be a better man, and to keep quiet about what had happened to him. But the leper raced over the countryside showing his new body and praising the marvelous man who had made him clean. The marveling leper could not hold his tongue, and this caused such a quake of excitement that Jesus could not go back into the town where the leper lived but had, again, to hide away. But still they found him.

In Peter's house—Peter and his wife were dear friends of Jesus' in Capernaum—an oddly beautiful thing happened. In order to avoid the crowds, Jesus had slipped back to Peter's house. Within minutes there were so many after Jesus that there was no room in the house or outside in the street. Jesus stood in one of the rooms of Peter's house and talked to all those around him. Suddenly a man in a bed floated down before him. When Jesus looked up he saw a hole in the roof and four men lowering the bed with ropes—they had torn away a part of the roof of Peter's house in order to get the paralyzed man to Jesus. The astonished Jesus was so impressed with the ingenuity of the four men and the determination of the paralyzed man that he said to him "May your sins be forgiven!" Some doubters were among the crowd in the room and they called out that it was a blasphemy that Jesus dared take it upon himself to forgive another man's sins, only God could do that. The paralyzed man humbly begged Jesus to forgive his starting an argument and told him that he had only been desperate to walk again and so had sought Jesus' hand. "Very well," Jesus said, "get up, carry the bed they brought you in, and go home." The paralyzed man did just that, overjoyed. Peter's house surely rocked with the cries of amazement, from the people in this room. Jesus had gained more disciples and more enemies. He amazed and thrilled some and irritated others among the people of Capernaum. His success was mixed.

He went on, to the lakeside. As he went on, he faced a customs officer named Levi; he looked at Levi and said, "Come with me." Levi went. They went to Levi's house. A gathering of all kinds of people was there. Immediately he was asked by his critics why he should be there among such people, sinners and crooks, and furthermore, why would he associate with people like Levi, a corrupt customs officer, and eat and drink in his house. Jesus said, "I came for the bad ones. They are the ones who need help and forgiveness, not the righteous. People who are not ill," he added, "do not need the doctor."

Jesus was causing such commotion that it was apparent to his enemies that some way had to be found to trap him. They began to try to trick him with subtle questions, and to catch him off guard. They watched for weak moments in him when he might be distracted and could be thrown off balance. If they could get something on him in public they would show him up before the adoring and entranced people around him. But the man was too quick and too shrewd for them. Jesus seemed, now, even to dare his opponents and his doubters by taking greater and greater risks with them. He was really closing in on *them*. More and more he was forcing *their* hand. This was his strategy. In a church on a Sabbath, shortly after the Levi incident, a man with a withered hand came to him. Now, it was a law that no one was to be healed on the Sabbath, and particularly in a church—obviously a foolish law in the eyes of a man like Jesus, and he commented, "The Sabbath was made for man, and not man for the Sabbath." (Mark 2:27) Therefore all eyes were on Jesus to see what he would do. In the hush Jesus was angry and demanded why they watched him so closely, was he a thief? Were you supposed to do good things on Sabbath days or evil things? he cried out. Save life or kill? The crowd was hushed. Stretch out your hand, he told the man; and he healed the withered hand.

This was enough for the Pharisees. They had not only watched this man defy the Law, but had been put down by him, before the people. They went to Herod's counselors and demanded their help in planning a way to catch and kill the man. (To want to kill Jesus for breaking the sacred law of the Sabbath was not, as it might seem, an extreme action. In the Old Testament Book of Numbers (15:32–36), read:

And while the children of Israel were in the wilderness, they found a man that gathered sticks upon the sabbath day. And they that found him gathering sticks brought him unto Moses and Aaron, and unto all the congregation. And they put him in ward, because it was not declared what should be done to him. And the Lord said unto Moses, The man shall be surely put to death; all the congregation shall stone him with stones without the camp. And all the congregation brought him without the camp, and stoned him with stones, and he died. . . .

In this critical moment Jesus fled with his four disciples to the lake. But by now, word of the great things he had done, of his defiance of the authorities and the establishment, of his wonders in healing, had spread all over Galilee and the neighboring province of Judea, and crowds were now coming to him even from Jerusalem, from beyond Jordan, and even from the far places of Tyre and Sidon. There were so many clamoring just to touch him, crying out "You are the son of God!" that he was afraid he would be crushed under their feet, and so he had to have a boat ready at the shore in case it became necessary to break free from the enraptured, if not hysterical, people. They called to him that he was a son of God and praised him for healing them (so many of those who had been healed by him never left him afterward but followed him wherever he went, as disciples; so that there was a band of deaf people who could now hear, blind people who could now see, and lamed who were leaping along the roads, behind him), saying we know that you are a teacher come from God, because no man can do such miracles unless God is with him. But he sternly ordered them not to make such a fuss of it, not even to make it known, and to keep his work quietly in their hearts. Jesus was keeping a secret, but it was more than keeping a secret: it was his knowledge of the dangerous situation he was in that made him implore his people to keep quiet. Sensationalism would bring him "success," and he was not looking for sensationalistic success. Success would be failure for him and would indeed endanger, if not ruin, his work.

The healing was causing the biggest problems now, but he could not turn away from those who came to him. But both healing and preaching were blasphemous, were traitorous. Blasphemous, in that he was taking on the authority that only God and the Pharisees and scribes and trustees of the Temple were granted. Traitorous, because he defied and broke the law, both religious and of the State. Therefore they sought to kill him because he had not only broken the Sabbath but had said that God was his father, which made him equal with God.

When Jesus said that unless a man be born again, he could not see the Kingdom of God, his opponents cried, "How dare you speak of the Kingdom of God, since you have no authority to do so? And, too, how dare you announce that the Kingdom of God is here now and available to everybody, when it is known that the Kingdom of God may be entered only by obeying strict laws—and besides, how can a man be born again when he is old? Can he enter the second time into his mother's womb and be born?"

There had been many disciples, committed followers of Jesus. A band of men and women had joined him as he went around, in addition to the four apostles Jesus had recruited earlier, but at a certain point he wanted to form a body of men that would constitute brotherhood, the nucleus of a movement that would spread over the world and change it. They would help him do his work and later go out to preach and help and heal. They would be twelve in number and they would be his apostles. These twelve men, all young men, simple men, men who worked with their hands as fishermen or carpenters, or artisans of some kind, men of all heart and simple needs, open-hearted and open-faced, these "Twelve," as they were to be called over and over in the Gospels, would form the inner circle of Jesus' movement and of his work; these twelve he would instruct and teach and show, so that they could carry on his work not only with him, but after him. There came to be many more "disciples"—followers and helpers and believers. At one point he chose seventy from the many who were with him, and sent them out over the nation to do special work and to open up the way for him. But at the moment he chose in addition to the first four (Peter, James, John and Andrew), eight more young men to make up the Twelve: Philip, Bartholomew, Matthew, Thomas, another James, Thaddeus, Simon, and Judas. These men loved Jesus totally, and they were his helpful, devoted brothers. What became of these men later, particularly Peter, who was called "The Rock" by Jesus and who was commissioned later by Jesus to become the very rock and foundation of his cause and his church and was given the "keys to the Kingdom," and is therefore, historically, considered the father of the established early Christian church? (He is the St. Peter of history, and he has often been painted and depicted with a chain of keys around his waist.) What became of men like Peter and James and John after Jesus was murdered and the cause went on without him is something to read. (The book of "The Acts of the Apostles" in the New Testament.) Peter did triumphant work in Rome after Jesus' death, and Mark, who wrote the little story of Jesus that bears his name—the Gospel of St. Mark—was there with Peter. It was Nero who later arranged for Peter's barbaric death in what was called "Nero's Circus" in the Colosseum. Others of the Twelve were stoned to death or hanged or crucified.

But in the beginning, with his Twelve and his many disciples, Jesus went swiftly along the way. Again he was mobbed by thousands. Luke reports in his Gospel of one instance "when there were gathered together an innumerable multitude of people, insomuch that they trode one upon another. . . ." (Luke 12:1) Some were now saying that he was mad, a fanatic, or simply trying to gain notoriety. Others said that Beelzebub, a classical and literal name for Satan, the Devil, was in Jesus, possessed him, and that the reason he was able to cast out devils in people was because he had the help of the Devil himself. This outraged Jesus, who called this accusation real blasphemy. How could Satan cast out Satan? How could Satan throw himself out of himself? If a house is divided against itself, it falls down, Jesus cried. Therefore, if Satan were to rise up against himself and so be divided, he could not stand, but would fall down.

While he was demonstrating his brilliance in all its power, someone came to tell him that his mother and his brothers and sisters were there and wanted to see him. He was annoyed with this. But who is my mother? he asked the thousands who were around him, and who are my brothers and sisters? You, he said to the great crowd, you are my mother and my brothers and my sisters; I belong to you (nowhere is Jesus' father, Joseph, mentioned; and he is presumed to have died early). You are my family, my kinfolk. We are told that his brothers and sisters and their mother, Mary, believed that he was out of his mind and should be brought home or given help. But what Jesus was feeling was quite the normal reaction of a young person functioning at his best. To be reminded of family affiliations at such a time is to be restricted, is to be made self-conscious. Such a son is doing a larger thing, a grander thing that surpasses all "relations" and has to do with only one relationship

—a kind of divine connection between him and the thing he is afire with.

He walked along the lake again, a favorite place of his for working among the people, talking and touching and making clean and calm and whole those who needed him. By this time he had little privacy except by stealing away to a mountain or desert hiding place; and little safety, where it was openly known that he was coming to be considered an outlaw. He was constantly slipping through the net of his pursuers as they tried to seize him, by darting away through the crowds. His enemies were many times at the point of stoning him. Jesus had become a fugitive. In reality, when we think about it, the greater part of his work was rarely done in a peaceful atmosphere. He had to work under pressure, against hecklers and rabble-rousers and spies. He had always been needled by smart questioners who wanted to show him up, heckled by those who wanted to make him angry, sharply challenged by other clever men who were no fools. In other words, this man's work was not at all a lovely sitting in a circle of sweet groves. It was done in peril, and swiftly, up and down the countryside, on roads and atop hills, in little villages for a while—but not for too long—in town churches, by the lake, in boats on the lake. In the smaller villages he was met by suspicious men. He was harassed on every turn. His life was a chase, and it swiftly became a deadly pursuit.

He got into most trouble with the holy authorities when he used the local synagogues for his own pronouncements and ideas. He was attacking stupidity and pretense where it originated and where it did the most harm—he was striking at the root. For instance, he flogged out of the Temple merchants who were selling sacrifice birds for the altar and changing street money to special church money—that is, you had to use a special kind of money that only the church sold to you, in order to make your offering. It was at this time that Jesus was saying, in the synagogues and in the presence of the priests and teachers, things like, If you give to the poor, don't make a big gesture as you do it, but do it so unnoticeably that your left hand doesn't even know that your right hand is doing it. The same for praying. Praying is leveling—the one time many people can level with themselves. Praying is not braying out in church or running a long tongue on street corners and hoping to be seen and heard by as many as possible. Flowery and wordy prayers make the loud-mouth and long-tongued think that the more they say the more they'll be heard—which is a waste of their time and of God's, and of other listeners. Do it briefly, simply, and privately. People want to hear just a few, good words. Jesus certainly practiced what he preached. If you read his great speeches you will find them spare and explosive in their tightly wound little bombs of truth.

He also said things like: Don't judge if you don't want to be judged yourself. Don't be so busy telling the other person that he has a speck in his eye when you have a whole clinker in yours, for it's obvious that you can only see the other person's speck when you remove the large obstruction to your own vision. And don't give foolishly of your precious own to the stupid and the self-concerned, thinking that you will gain something from them.

They'll only trample your pearls under their feet and then turn back upon you and trample *you*. If you ask for something you will get it. If you seek, you will find; and if you knock on a door, it will open. The man was giving free practical advice. Who had heard such simple true things before? The crowds doubled and doubled again. Once, we are told, when there were five thousand listeners in a "desert place" who had been with him all day without eating, he made it possible for that many people to eat a filling meal from five loaves of bread and two fish, and still there was enough left over to fill twelve baskets.

On he went. Such miracles did him no good with the law. The people were astounded, and even the Twelve were perplexed. They often asked him: What's this, Lord? What do you mean by that? Would you please clear up for us what you just told the people? Often he would be impatient with them and beg them just to use a little imagination. These are parables. They are simple in their meaning but they require a little thought, a little time, a little imagination. They are about the simplest things—a seed, a piece of bread, a vine, a sheep, a pitcher of water. If you listen to them as if they were high-flown poetry, he warned, then you are putting me in the same boat with the authorities of the official pulpits and "approved" speaking places; and you are comparing me with the scholars and the wise men who analyze and lip out high-sounding half-truths and dead rules that they call the Law.

The "Law" is simple, he said: "All things whatsoever you would that men should do to you, do you even so unto them." *This* is the what-you-call "Law," he said. Besides, you can tell what people are by what they produce—put up or shut up, to make it clear and plain. You will know the truth of them by what they put out from themselves, like fruit trees. Some put out thorns and thistles instead of grapes and figs. A good tree makes good fruit; a no-good one, no-good fruit.

And if you build a house on rock, winds and floods cannot break it down; but if you build on sand, obviously the house won't stand.

This was the way he talked to the people, to his

disciples, and the way he trained his Twelve apostles. He made them see life freshly—he was like a breath of fresh air—and they felt some hope and some life and some joy. They also followed him. More and more joined his company and his fellowship, becoming disciples. When he understood the woman who was caught in the act of making love to a married man and called an adulteress by her neighbors, and did not condemn her weakness, the woman was so surprised by his compassion (she might have been stoned to death by her neighbors —the plight of sinners in lust) and by his not judging her, that she asked who he could be and where was he going and said that wherever it was, she was going too, to be with him and serve him. She went, too, and followed him to the very cross at the end of his life. So that people were saying: Who is this man who not only heals us but forgives our weaknesses and mistakes too? He gave them a way where before they had none—or only half a way, or a lost way; it wasn't worth much; they only endured and hung on. And Jesus kept saying to them: Listen to me, I have shown you the way.

I am that way. I have come to save those who are lost and to show this way to the lost; you can begin again; you can be new; and I have come with my Word to the broken-hearted, the sick of heart and mind and body. I give you Life, I give you living water, living bread, an open door. Have faith in me, I am with *you*, each *one* of you, in everything you do.

Naturally they followed and clung to him and loved him. But others also pursued him in stealth, laid traps for him and plotted to try to kill him. The Pharisees cunningly tried to make him speak heresy, which would permit the Sanhedrin to take him as a blasphemer of the ancient Law or the Roman governor to condemn him as a revolutionary.

In Herod's prison John had been hearing of the works of Jesus. He sent two of his disciples to Jesus to make sure this was the same man. Jesus said: Go back and tell John that I am the man. Tell him that the blind see, the lame walk, the unclean are clean, the deaf hear, the dead are raised up, and the poor hear good news.

34

To hear again of his beloved brother John roused up strong feelings in Jesus, and he spoke stingingly to the crowd about John. Of course he's in prison, is what Jesus was crying out, because he is a man of courage and says what he believes and has no fear of telling the truth! John is a mighty man. When all of you went to the river in the wilderness to see and hear this man, what did you expect? Just a reed rustled by the wind, a piping little voice? You heard a roar! What did you go to the river to see—a soft man in soft clothes like some dandy, some dance master in a king's palace? What did you go to see out there by the river—a magician and fortune-teller, a prophet? Well that's what you saw, and more than that: a man of love and fury who prepared the way for me to come here and do my work.

He scolded the world for maligning and abusing John. He seemed close to insurrection. He was on fire and cried out against those who had attacked him and criticized him and against those in power and authority who had said that John was mad, and that he, Jesus, was an evil man and devil-bound. But then after this outpouring he quieted and added: But never mind, come to me if you are heavy with troubles and struggles and I'll give you some rest because, despite my outrage, I am "meek and lowly in heart"; and I'll give you rest and peace. "Take my yoke upon you, and learn of me."

Not long after, John was slaughtered like a beast. Herod had John's head cut off and brought in on a food platter to a drunken supper party celebrating his birthday; and only to please the whim of a dancing girl named Salome. But John's destiny was in Jesus, and all through Jesus' work people kept asking and wondering if Jesus was John arisen —even Herod, who later was terrified that Jesus was John come back again, so much was John's spirit living and working in Jesus.

It was a time of terror and terrorism. The murder of John was such a bestial act and so disturbing to Jesus that it might have set him and his disciples into a rebellion. But, no, it was not the time, nor was it Jesus' way.

So many sorrows and disappointments, disillusionments and losses were now falling upon him.

He had gone home to Nazareth to teach and heal there, to see old friends, perhaps to show his hometown what he had become; but they laughed at him, they thought he was putting on airs or perhaps was a little out of his wits. Few paid him any attention. He was shocked and hurt and said that a prophet is without honor and recognition only in his own country and in his own house and among his own kin. He left home again.

It was time to rearrange things. Jesus had been rejected, challenged, and threatened. More and more his spectacular healing was his drawing power; his teachings seemed to be secondary. The people wanted a "Messiah," a hero-Savior-king, all in one. A clouding sense of failure began to gather over Jesus. He had had a plan; the community he had envisioned was not increasing on all sides. His enemies were increasing. People were not turning to his new way, were not repenting. Some did not seem convinced that the Kingdom of God was at hand; they wanted the Kingdom of Israel restored, and others wanted more wonders. The wrong kind of excitement was quivering through the thousands who followed and thronged him.

Frustrated and dissatisfied, he called his apostles together and announced a new plan of action. They would go out, two by two, over the country and spread his news. They would go humbly and under the utmost self-sacrifice, taking nothing for the journey but the clothes on their backs and the shoes on their feet. The time had come for the spreading of Jesus' message. The Twelve would meet and teach and help the people, eating and sleeping in whatever homes they were invited into.

These twelve young men were met with not a little coldness and often outright disfavor, and their mission was not too successful. Into a world of hopelessness, one of cheating and hating and killing, of illness, emptiness of heart, days of meaningless drudgery, came these simple men, bringing love and hope, and pressing for action—now. Jesus' action appears now to have become a rather urgent campaign, a planned overthrowing of the old structures, a planned revolt, even. Because of its impetus, its building swiftness and daring, its increasing awareness of enemies, the invasion of Jesus' twelve messengers had not only the quality of impassioned evangelism, but moved with an air of pursuit, avoiding enemy territory and plotting quick escape if necessary. Once again it is evident that Jesus' ministry was not a gentle plateau action, a benevolent crusade. His ministry had taken shape as a driving action thrust forward by a sense of limited time. Had not both John the Baptist and Jesus, the insurrectionists, known from the beginning that their work was going to be radical and anarchical? ("He who is not with me is against me"; "I have come to set men at variance"); an uncompromising and unsettling encounter, stirring up a revolution within each man? Moreover, had they not known that it was going to be an open challenge of authority, an intentional violation of rules, a deliberate breaking up and overturning of the old stale and unjust order, to free humanity from the bondage of the stupid and the cunning, and to set example and establish precedent for the very "Kingdom"? This new haunting stranger among men was not just a sweet wandering preacher. He had an edge of mystic fervor on him, a quality of restrained fury and of dark hidden power, of burning love and suffering in him. In a man of such compassion and forgiveness it was obvious to those who came in touch with him that there was, nevertheless, little room for compromise or maudlin politeness in him.

After a while they returned, the Twelve, to report to Jesus. He had been staying around the lakeside towns. Their news was discouraging, and once again Jesus knew that his Galilean campaign had not succeeded as he had dreamt it. A new sadness overcame him—but a new fierceness as well. He upbraided the towns that had rejected and disregarded him; he even called down destruction upon these towns (Matt. 11:20–24); but he went on with his Twelve and his disciples, while once again thousands blocked his way with cots of sick people; and they nearly stampeded to try to touch the hem of his robe, in the hope that they might be restored.

The Pharisees were busier than ever, trying to find fault and to catch him. They began "to urge him vehemently, and to provoke him to speak of many things; laying wait for him and seeking to catch something out of his mouth, that they might accuse him." (Luke 11:53–54) Once they saw him and his disciples eating without having washed their hands. The lawmakers denounced the man for not holding to the tradition of the elders and for breaking the old Law. Jesus was quite quick-tempered now and was often impatient, snapping back at critics and goaders. His tongue had gotten quicker and sharper, and his lashing denunciations of the scribes and Pharisees were dazzling in their brilliant fury. He called them hypocrites who honored the Law with lips and not hearts: ". . . ye pay tithe of mint and anise and cummin, and have omitted the weightier matters of the law, judgment, mercy and faith." They strained out a gnat from their drink and yet swallowed a camel. They were like "whited sepulchers," which appear outwardly beautiful but inside are full of dead men's bones. They were serpents, they were a generation of vipers; and they would not escape the damnation of hell. (Matt. 23:23–33) Their doctrines were meaningless and absurd and had nothing to do with life. For love and faith, he spat out, you substitute washing hands and cups and pots. Jesus went into a tirade and called all the people around to hear him say that he hoped everyone there understood that it was his belief that anything that goes into a man from the outside cannot corrupt him. But the things that come *out* of him, from the inside, are what really corrupt him and make him evil.

When he and his disciples had left the people some of them said that they didn't quite get the message in the parable that he had just told the people. Jesus was again irritated and said: Are you, too, so blind of understanding? Can't you see that I meant that what goes into a man from the outside goes into his belly and not his heart; while what comes out of him from within, from his heart, are such things as greed, envy, arrogance, deceit, pride?

This time of fury marks a big turn in Jesus' life. He was taking a definite stand before his enemies. He was revealing the depths of his temperament, new qualities of his mind. He was tired of being hounded and picked at, mobbed, idealized, mauled, and constantly nagged. Once again he withdrew, this time to the northern borders of Tyre and Sidon. He went into a house and withdrew, seeking privacy. Once again he had to re-evaluate, to get a fresh sense of himself and an idea of what to do next. Yet still they were after him, bringing the afflicted, and especially one who was deaf and had an impediment in his speech. Jesus took him aside and "put his fingers into his ears, and he spit, and touched his tongue." Then Jesus said, "Be opened. And straightway his ears were opened, and the string of his tongue was loosed, and he spake plain." (Mark 7:32–37) And still Jesus instructed these astounded whole and renewed people not to tell anybody. But how could they help it? ". . . the more he charged them, so much the more a great deal they published it," reports Mark, "and were beyond measure astonished."

He seems to have been shuttling back and forth on the lake to evade and escape the notorious crowd and the ever-present danger of the Pharisees closing in on him like a posse. Once they caught him again and questioned him and demanded that he give them a sign from heaven to guarantee who he was. The man "sighed deeply in his spirit" and would not give in and asked: Why don't you believe me; why does this generation demand a sign? There will be none beyond what I have already shown. And he escaped in a boat across the lake, warning his disciples to be more than ever careful of the Pharisees and of Herod. He was less patient, these days, being under such constant harassment. When his companions didn't understand one of his statements, he scoffed at them, saying: Don't you have eyes? Don't you have ears? Can't you remember anything? Can't you understand anything?

They came into one of the lake towns, Bethesda, where a charming little incident of healing took place. It was of a blind man. When Jesus had spat on his hands and put them on the blind man's eyes and asked him if he saw anything, the blind man looked up and said "I see men as trees, walking." This obviously was an incomplete healing, and

Jesus tried again. This time the man looked up and saw "every man clearly."

Now he asked his disciples who people were saying he was. Some said John the Baptist, they answered; yet some said he was one of the great prophets like Elijah. But Peter said: you are the Christ, the son of God! Jesus said: I am, but I charge you not to tell this to anyone. This must be a secret. Jesus went on to say that, furthermore, he had more news for the Twelve, something more to prepare them for, and that was that he was going to have to suffer more and more, and that his enemies would finally catch him and kill him; but not for long. After three days, he said, I shall be among you again. Peter was startled and angry and didn't want to hear any more of this talk. These young followers would not believe this kind of talk from Jesus. But Jesus was now getting deeper insight into his destiny, more clearly understanding the way he had to go; and all he could say to his apostles was that they were thinking about his life in terms of earthly things, "things that be of men." It is strange and human and yet sad that these

Twelve could never believe that Jesus was going to be killed and then get his life back again. But the point is that by this time the man had come to see his way as one of suffering—but of *suffering through* to joy. His victory, his triumph would come—but in another way, and one that had "not been generally known." Jesus was trying to make this clear to his brothers, but they could not accept or really understand. Even when he took Peter, James, and John up on the mountain with him and demonstrated his mystical nature, his spiritual identity, in what is called the Transfiguration, they were frightened and puzzled, and simply could not understand. In the moment of Transfiguration, Jesus appeared before Peter, James, and John in a shining whiteness as though he were all alight, and it is written that a voice said of Jesus, "This is my beloved Son; Hear him." So the Transfiguration, however one wishes to look at it in terms of mystical truth, spiritual revelation, or whatever, really was simply an official announcement of Jesus' identity, as a special man among men. Afterward Jesus told his three companions not to tell anybody of what they had seen until he had risen from the dead. Peter, James, and John kept wondering together what "risen from the dead" could mean. Jesus tried to explain that it was intended that the Son of Man must come and suffer many things, be counted for nothing, and that the powers would do to him what they pleased. He would prevail, however, and after three days in the ground rise alive forever. The men were bewildered.

As the four came down from the strange happening on the mountain, they found a mob of people running around excitedly. When Jesus asked what the trouble was, they answered that an unfortunate and embarrassing thing had happened. Some of the disciples had failed in trying to rid a man's son of a "dumb spirit." The father of the boy was disturbed and told Jesus that his son had been tormented by such problems since he was born, that he often "foamed and gnashed" and would even throw himself into fire or water. Please have mercy and help us, the man begged Jesus. Jesus, impatient and tired, reminded his disciples that they had failed because they lacked sufficient faith. "O faithless generation!" he cried out. "How long shall I be with you, how long shall I suffer?" To the man he said: If you have faith and belief, then all things are possible. The man cried out in tears: "Lord, I believe! Help me in my unbelief." The bad thing in the young man came out of him at Jesus' challenge, and left him still. Again Jesus begged that no one tell of the incident.

Now, as Jesus and his disciples were moving swiftly about Galilee in and out of the towns around the lake, he was teaching them more intensely about what was meant by the "Son of God," instructing them again and again that he would fall into the hands of men and be killed by them, but that on the third day after he was killed he would be raised up. And once again they did not understand him, and were afraid to ask him what he meant.

These were strange, intense times; there was something dark and mystic and unsettling in the air. Jesus moved more furtively and spoke more emotionally. He sounded now sometimes embittered and defeated. He was saying that humanity persecutes and destroys what it most hungers for. Again he upbraided the cities where he had performed most of his mighty work, and he went so far as to curse and damn them. And then, having said these fierce things, he fell back into the gentle visionary man that he was, a man of such good hope and who had walked along with such good news for everybody; and in spite of all his bitterness and his disillusionment, he finished in love by saying "Come unto me, all ye that labor and are heavy-laden, and I will give you rest. Take my yoke upon you, and learn of me; for I am meek and lowly in heart; and ye shall find rest unto your souls. For my yoke is easy and my burden is light."

What had kept him from his fullness, this now hunted and marked man? What had prevented him from bringing the total brotherhood into being? Many people wanted to see him as a political king, a popular Messiah. Others meant to place him in the royal line of descendants from David, the first great Hebrew king. But Jesus was under divine commission because he had been touched with the Spirit and turned to his mission on the day he was baptized. He wasn't going to get caught in a political situation. The more he spoke of his good news, his glad tidings, the more the people asked if he was not the Messiah come to free Israel from bondage, if he was not the son of David come to save the people at last. When he rejected these titles and spoke of another King and another Kingdom, that other salvation and that other freedom, the people—and often his disciples and many apostles, too—were bewildered or hostile. The circle was narrowing; his enemies were closing in upon him, posing shrewder questions: Was it "lawful" in his opinion that a man do this or that? And he answered more and more daringly, "All things are told to me of my father; and no man knoweth the son but the father; neither knoweth any son the father, save the son, and he to whomsoever the son will reveal himself."

"Therefore they sought the more to kill him,

because he . . . said that God was his own father, making himself equal with God." (John 5:18)

It was Passover time and now they were going to Jerusalem, and Jesus warned his twelve close brothers that he would be betrayed, scourged and beaten, condemned to death, and killed. They were awed by his strange dark new sense of himself; and they were afraid, too; for the whole approach to Jerusalem had been ominous and frightening; and Jesus' tragic sense of the moment scared them and bewildered them. Somewhere in the advance toward the great city was the feeling of an invasion, of an attack, of a "march." He said things that gave them a sense of last times, of things ending, of farewell. Like, "whoever of you will be the leader will be the follower; the master will be the servant. For the son of man came in order to serve, not to be served." Peter, James, John and the others could not understand this. They still hoped for an earthly Kingdom and one in which they would have an important place. James and John had already asked Jesus if they could "sit on either side of him" when he attained the power that would be his! This had made the other apostles angry, and they considered their brothers self-seeking and competitive, and all complained to Jesus—who quietened them by answering that power and status were not his to give.

Now they were almost at Jerusalem. There was a tremendous sense of event. At the outskirts of the town Jesus sent two disciples for a colt that had been prearranged for; and he rode into the city on the colt. This could have meant many things: that he was not a "king" who would have ridden into the city on a grand stallion, for instance, for he was coming into the great city as a humble man on the meekest of beasts. Jesus also had a sense of the spectacle. Jerusalem was jammed with pilgrims and tourists at Passover, for it was a festival time. He wanted to catch the eyes of the crowds and also impress upon his enemies that he meant business. His entrance then was deliberately and cleverly dramatized. It was an announcement of his identity. The crowds loved it (". . . all the city was moved, saying, Who is this? And the multitude said, This is Jesus the Prophet of Nazareth, of Galilee."). (Matt. 21:10–11) And they waved branches and strew leaves and branches before him and helped make it a grand and triumphal arrival. The apostles, who had seen so much, simple men who had been witness to so many dramatic happenings and wonders since they first joined this man, had never dreamt of such a time of glory as this. In all of this, auspicious and dangerous as it was, Jesus kept his simple sense of the human: seeing a short man standing up in a tree at the side of the road, Jesus realized that the man was too short to see the little parade from the side of the street. Jesus stopped the procession and greeted the short man in the tree and invited him down to join the procession.

When Jesus entered Jerusalem he was entering a world, a nation that had long been expecting, according to legend and prophecy, a political leader —a "Messiah"—who would save their country from the ills of bondage, injustice, and corruption. We know that Jesus was not this kind of Savior-Messiah—he was the Savior-man, the Savior of each man, unique unto himself. If he was the "Son of God" it was in the sense of being a servant to every man, of being every man's "Son." His hurt and his loss were that many did not see this— yet; not even his own twelve companions. Yet he had already explained the bitter truth that only if he went all the way to his death, gave up his life, would his true meaning be known. This is what he knew as he sat astride the never-before-ridden colt and proceeded with those following him—including the short man he had invited down from the tree—into the holy and doomed city of Jerusalem.

He was *arriving*. This man who could be so meek (even as his sitting on a humble beast symbolized) was announcing himself as a figure of authority. What a difference between the Jesus who came out of the water that John had led him into, and the Jesus now entering Jerusalem! His human growth had been fostered and enriched by the people he had touched and loved. How far he had come since the day of his baptism and through his moving among men in human experience! He had come to a full, mature, tragic sense of himself, to a vision of his destiny, to the full force of his authority. He had confronted his true identity in the world, he had accepted the demands of his destiny beyond the world, although it had been bitter to accept the cup. And although it had already been made known to him, he had had to earn his destiny, he had had to suffer for it. Through the revelation of the Spirit, and through the open-hearted faith of the humblest men and women, through living encounters with the living, he had strengthened his own faith and accepted himself, this up-to-that-moment regional man, unknown in the great world beyond his local lakes and mountains, in his early thirties and whose life on earth would be so brief and yet move, living and real, through the ages.

Having come into the city, he observed it with sorrow and wonder, and, since it was nightfall, went outside the city, beyond the village of Bethany, with his disciples.

The next morning his onslaught on the city was like an attack in its ferocity and swiftness. It was close to terrorist action against the law and the magistrates. Jerusalem—one of the great, rich, ghetto-breeding cities that we know about so well —was exploiting tourists and pilgrims at the festival time of Passover. The Sadducees were a religious and political aristocracy that had literally taken over the priesthood and controlled and commercialized the whole machinery of temple sacrifices and offerings (doves were sold for sacrifices on the altar, and there was special money that the pilgrim, the tourist-worshiper had to buy and could buy only in the Temple, in order to make the required monetary offering). The Sadducees were little concerned with the spiritual needs of the people, but they enforced special laws of feasts and sacrifice at Jerusalem.

It was this situation, this established order and custom in Jerusalem, that Jesus marched right in on that morning. A trap was already laid for him: his enemies would cause him to speak heresy. The Sanhedrin, the official council and court of appeals for all questions involving Mosaic Law, and a powerful machine made up of chief priests, scribes (experts in the Law and the interpretation of the Law in the light of tradition), and elders (tribal and family heads of the priesthood and the people—the secular nobility of Jerusalem), had the right of capital punishment; but confirmation of the Roman governor was necessary to pass sentence of death. If Jesus could be made to speak heresy, this would permit the Sanhedrin to seize him as a blasphemer in the name of the law of Moses, or the Roman governor, Pontius Pilate, to condemn him as a revolutionary.

During these few days in the capital it seems clear that the man was engaged in acts of terrorism against corruption and injustice. He swept into the Temple and overturned the tables of the money-changers and the stalls where the doves were sold. The money was scattered over the floor, and the doves flew. He threw out anybody who was buying and selling within the Temple. He made such a scene and caused such a furor inside and outside the great Temple in Jerusalem that the crowds ran to him and there was a near-riot. Jesus was trying to drive everybody to decisive action, people and politicians and church authorities. His sense of his destiny and his urgent mission was now at its highest and most furious, and it was combined with his sense of his own personal danger and the necessity of giving his life for what had to be done right here and now. Once again, the hand of John the Baptist, full of river water, on his head only some months ago, blessed him and urged him on.

Who was he to do such things in the holy Temple of Jerusalem? He preached much like John the Baptist at this moment. And at the height of his almost fanatical passion, outraged by swindling and cheating, he declared that the very building of that great city, the very walls, would be thrown down, stone by stone. He railed at the rulers and shouted to the people gathered in the courts of the Temple that they had their rights and that he was there to defend their rights; and to throw out the bagmen and the ghetto lords and the moneymen in the temples. The people were shocked at his boldness but swarmed around him, and there was pandemonium. Jesus was on fire and was driving on, and the scribes and chief priests were afraid that there was going to be a rebellion and were trying to devise ways to kill this man. He left the city and went back to his friends' house in Bethany to rest for the night.

The next morning he was right in there again and was at once cornered by the chief priests and the scribes and the elders. They demanded to know by what authority Jesus had come in here and done these things. Jesus, whose powers were at their height, answered that if they could tell him whether they believed that John's baptizing was man-conceived or God-conceived, he would tell them what his authority was. The religious men were at a standstill, for if they said that John's baptism came from heaven, then this would be an acceptance of Jesus; and if it came from man, then the people who were crowded around them and listening with all ears would turn on the priests and the scribes and the elders, since they all believed that John was indeed a prophet. Those in authority were blocked and could not give an answer. Neither will I give an answer, therefore, said Jesus, and he had outwitted them—and before the crowds, who roared with approval.

To the crowd, now, and before his enemies and opponents, Jesus began a long and vivid speaking. He told parables, the one about the vineyard, ending with the beautiful little truth: "The stone which the builders rejected is become the head of the corner." (Mark 12:10) His enemies knew that this parable was directed at them, and they were now murderous and determined to kill him; but, again, they were afraid of the people. His enemies went off and got together a little group of their brightest Pharisees and the toughest men from Herod's group to try to catch Jesus at words that would be incriminating enough to justify a death sentence. This time the question was, since you tell the truth at any cost and in fear of no man, could you tell us whether you believe in the law that enforces us to pay poll tax to Caesar—is it fair? Well, Jesus said, let me see a coin. When they showed him a coin on which there was an inscription and a face, Jesus said: Whose face is this, and what is this written on the coin? The man answered that the face was Caesar's. Well then, give Caesar what is his and give God what is his. Just don't get them mixed up. This answer dumfounded the questioners, although it was close to treason in the minds of some. But there were other questions and other questioners. They were all at him and it was like a huge and tumultuous debate with thousands all around listening and watching. There were questions about resurrection, to which Jesus answered: "He is not the God of the dead, but the God of the living. Who's interested in the dead? We are concerned with the living. You make mistakes all around, and this is because you don't know the Scriptures—which is your business and the basis of the so-called authority which you use against men." This was insult and the rankest blasphemy, since these men represented the spiritual law and leadership. There was one young scribe who had been impressed with Jesus' answers, and he came up and humbly asked the question: "Which is the first commandment of all?" To which he got one of the most beautiful sayings of Jesus: "The Lord our God is one Lord. And thou shalt love the Lord your God with all thy heart, and all thy soul, and with all thy mind, and with all thy strength: this is the first commandment and the second is alike, namely this, thou shalt love thy neighbor as thyself. There is none other commandment greater than this." (Mark 12:29–31) This young scribe came close to being changed to Jesus' way of thinking because he answered that he agreed with the beautiful things Jesus had said, that there is only one God for us all no matter who we are, that to love him with all the heart and with all the understanding and with all the soul and with all the strength and to love his neighbor as himself is more than all the burnt offering and sacrifices in the world. Jesus might have had another disciple right there, had it not been so dangerous a moment. For Jesus went on criticizing the hypocrites and he got absolutely specific in his accusation—so much so, that it is amazing that he was not assassinated on that day. Had he been assassinated there would have been a riot to match some of the most violent in history, for by now the whole city was stirred up by this spellbinding man and near a kind of hysteria that holidays cause. Now he was sparing nothing: Beware of these men you have heard challenging me today, they love to go around in impressive clothes of flowing robes and say their "Bless you's!" as they walk sanctimoniously in the market place. Notice, he said, that they always sit in the best seats in church, have the best of everything at feasts, swindle widows out of their houses, and mouth out long prayers.

As they, Jesus and his Twelve—who had never dreamt of coming so triumphantly into this lavish and splendid city and who were in awe of their leader and afraid for him and for themselves, too —left the Temple and the square where this decisive thing had just happened, one of them said, "Master, see what manner of stones and what buildings are here!" This gave Jesus an opportunity to prophesy that all would fall to the ground under men's own hands in war, in hatred, and in violence. Now he led Peter, James, John, and Andrew, his very first brothers whom he chose that day when he first began his work as he walked along the lake and found them in their work there (what things had happened; what wonders they had seen since that day they first left everything behind them and went along with this man—and not so long ago either, although it might have seemed years ago), he led his first four brothers away with him for a time to a spot on the Mount of Olives near the great Temple he had cursed and condemned. He wanted especially to tell them some things. And they had questions. Lord, they asked, what does all this mean? Something is going to happen. Can you give us any sign of what is ahead for us? Jesus said: I want to warn you that there will be many pseudo-Christs and false prophets who will come along and deceive people. This is one of your tasks, to rout them. Also, as my followers, let me tell you that you are going to be abused, harmed, beaten, mocked and constantly questioned—all these for my sake and because you were with me and believed in me and worked with me. But when you are questioned and tried, don't worry about your answers; they will come to you easily and without strain: they will come from me. Endure and work and believe, is what he was telling them. But as he spoke to them, four simple, full-hearted men who loved him, he was suddenly speaking to the world, and he spoke afire and ablaze with prophetic speech, ending simply with the advice: "Watch and Pray." This fiery and visionary speech can be read in the 13th Chapter of St. Mark.

Now it was time for the Feast of the Passover. All Jerusalem, teeming with tourists and pilgrims, was preparing for the feast of unleavened bread. Jesus was planning to eat the Passover feast with his Twelve; and his enemies were planning how to seize him and kill him. For although it was now determined that Jesus would be killed, the decision had been made to wait until the feast day was over "lest there be an uproar of the people." Yet they still had not found a way to catch the man. Suddenly a way was offered them by one of the very Twelve, Judas Iscariot. Judas would take them to Jesus after the supper, for a price: thirty silver pieces. It was agreed.

Jesus and the Twelve arranged for supper to be

eaten in a large upper room of somebody's house. It was there, as they were eating together, that Jesus spoke to them of the fellowship, the brotherhood, the community that they had begun not so long ago but that had taken them through so much, and he spoke to them not of the past, but of the future. Yet he was speaking a farewell, he was saying goodbye, he was showing them what they had to do without him and he was comforting and consoling and assuring them. These simple, good, totally loving young men could not understand. They could not understand his sorrowful words, nor his grief. Why was he leaving them? Where was he going? What was going to happen to him? What would *they* do? This eating together and drinking wine together was the celebration of all that these men had come through together, of all the work they had done together, of the wonders they had seen and witnessed and done, with each other's help. It was the end of all that.

But they didn't know that it was the end. And when Jesus suddenly said, one of you is going to betray me to my enemies here in the city of Jerusalem, the men could not believe that it was possible, and each one of them assured Jesus that it was not going to be he. Who was it? Who could it be? And Jesus, knowing what they did not know, broke the bread and shared it tenderly with them and passed the wine and they drank it together; and he told them that bread and wine would be broken and drunk in memory of him forever after. This, the Last Supper, was a parting that was to become reunion, over and over again, through the centuries.

After supper they all went to the Mount of Olives nearby. There was now such a finality in the air and such protestations and promises and comfortings, and every time Jesus talked about those who would fail him, it was Peter, above all, who could not bear him to speak of such things. Yet Jesus reminded him that he, Peter, would betray their friendship three times during the very coming night. Peter was angry and hurt when he heard this and he cried out that he would not do such a thing in any possible way that could be imagined.

The others all agreed. In this state of suspicion and in a strange quivering air of anxiety they all came into a garden on the side of the mountain, called Gethsemane. Jesus told his friends to stay there while he went off a little way to pray. He was going through the pain of suffering for himself which the others did not understand. He asked Peter, James, and John to come along with him into the garden. He told them very plainly that his soul was "exceeding sorrowful unto death"; and he asked them to linger behind but not to leave while he went on ahead a little to be by himself. He had asked them to be alert and to "keep a watch."

He went off by himself and the man fell on the ground and again cried out that he was afraid and that he hoped, being a man and frail, and loving the world and the men and women in it as he did, that if it were possible the terrible thing that was coming to him might be spared him. He actually asked his Father if he would reconsider. He went through the kind of torment that every human being has felt unbearable and, in his humanity, has quietly asked if there just might be a chance that he did not have to go through it. I don't know how I am going to do it, was the man's cry. But, he added, whatever I have to do I will do, since in my faith I see that it is not my choice, but yours, my Father.

In this bitter time, this time of dreadful aloneness, he needed his brothers. He went to them, if only for comfort, and he found them asleep. He shook them and asked, could you not stay awake for me even one hour? The men were exhausted and tried to answer, but only mumbled. I know you meant well, he told them, and I know that although the spirit means well, the flesh is weak, the body is the problem. He went off again and prayed. When he came back the second time they were again asleep, Peter, John, and James. He said the same thing to them, but stupefied with fatigue, they could not answer him. They were simply very tired men and they did not know truly what was going on. The man Jesus was that much alone. When he came back the third time and found them still asleep, he resigned himself and he said to them, Don't wake now, sleep on and take your rest. It is enough, the hour is come. What he meant was:

You couldn't help or save me anyhow, even though I thought you might, and even though I needed you so much. But what I forgot is that you are beloved humanity, dear mortality. Get up, he said, and let us go. What I had hoped you'd watch out for, has come while you slept—those who will kill me. And here they are.

While the three apostles were rubbing their eyes and trying to wake up, a group of men with knives and clubs came out of the shadows, and leading them was Judas himself. It was agreed that Judas would indicate the man they wanted by kissing him. Judas went straight to Jesus and kissed him, and that was when they seized him.

One of the apostles drew his sword and cut off the ear of one of the captors. It was a violent moment, a moment of gangsters and murderers. But Jesus said to the man with the sword: Don't use the sword; and to the man who took him he said: In all the times you wanted to take me, why didn't you? Day after day I was with you in the Temple teaching, and you did not seize me. Why did you have to come for me, armed and in the night, as though I were a thief?

He was left in the hands of his captors. All but one of his apostles fled into the darkness. Only two people lingered nearby as they bound Jesus to take him away. A mysterious young man, wrapped in a cloth, rushed out of the shadows and tried to grab Jesus from his captors. (Some have said it was young Mark.) When they laid hold of the young man he slipped out of the cloth and ran away, naked, in the night. Peter hid back in the shadows. Jesus was led away in the middle of the night to a place where the high priest and the chief priests and all the elders and the scribes were waiting for him. It was very well arranged. Peter followed stealthily at a distance and even went into the palace of the high priest where they took his beloved friend, and "warmed himself at the fire" in the courtyard.

The band of ruffians who had been hired by the Jewish High Court of Justice, called the Sanhedrin, brought him before the High Priest Caiaphas and all the authorities of the Sanhedrin, the official council of the Jews, who were assembled and waiting for him. The whole council asked for evidence against Jesus, so that he could be condemned to death. Although there had seemed to be so many witnesses against him before, only false witnesses stood up and accused him. A few stood up and said they had heard him say that he would tear down the Temple of Jerusalem that was made with hands and build up another in three days without human hands; but there weren't enough supporting witnesses to reinforce this charge and it seemed too weak and absurd a testimony to convict a man to death.

Now that they had caught him, they had to be firm and final. But so far, the witnesses had contributed nothing; their evidence had no substance. The high priest then asked Jesus if he had anything to say in the face of these words. Jesus "held his peace" and said nothing. Then the high priest asked him if he was the Christ "the Son of the Blessed"? Jesus said, "You say I am." And then he added: "You will see the Son of Man sitting at the right hand of Power, and coming in the clouds of heaven." The high priest tore his clothes in rage and cried out, What else? This is enough! This is blasphemy! Now, what do you all say to this? Clearly guilty, they answered, and some of them spat on Jesus and others hit him in the face and knocked him down.

Peter was lurking behind in the shadowy courtyard of the palace, not knowing what to do. The others had fled, and yet he could not. While he was waiting, a young woman thought she recognized him as one of the friends of Jesus. She said, Haven't I seen you with the man upstairs? Peter said not only had she *not* seen him, but that he didn't even understand what she was talking about. *What man?* A cock crowed. Not much later another young woman saw him there and told the others, he's one of them. Peter denied again. And a little while later during that long night, somebody said to Peter, You are one of the Galileans because you even talk like them. This time Peter cursed and swore at them and told them to let him alone and not to associate him with the man in trouble. I don't know this man you are talking about! he cried out. He heard the cock crow the second time and he remembered the words of Jesus that before the cock would crow twice Peter would deny him three times. Remembering this, Peter wept bitterly. It was a long and horrible night.

In the morning the authorities bound Jesus and took him to Pontius Pilate, the Roman governor. Pilate asked him outright: "Are you the King of the Jews?" Jesus said: That's what you say. Those are your words. Pilate could not get Jesus to say anything, and he was impressed with the man's dignity and self-control. He obviously did not feel the man was guilty of anything serious and tried to avoid having to indict him by offering up to the people a murderer named Barabbas as a replacement for Jesus. But no one would have a replacement; the people wanted the life of Jesus; it was too late and too wild and there was too much violence and vengeance underneath everything. And so, despite his wife's dream about the innocence of Jesus and his own sense of it in the man, Pontius Pilate, afraid of Caesar and afraid of the people, turned away and washed his hands of the affair and allowed the accusers of Jesus to decree that he be nailed to a cross and left hanging there until dead. The charges against him were blasphemy (giving himself the title "Son of Man"), sedition (threatening to destroy the Temple), and treason (proclaiming himself King).

Luke reports that Pilate shunted Jesus over to the house of Herod Antipas. Herod, in Jerusalem for the Feast of Passover, had heard of Jesus with curiosity. He also had some fear that this man might be John risen from the dead, as some had said. Herod only played with the pathetic bound and beaten and condemned man. Pitiful in his toying childishness, he asked for a "miracle" as though it were an amusing divertissement. Since no "sign" came forth from the strange, silent man before him, Herod pushed him away as though he were a boring toy.

Jesus was taken away and humiliated by the soldiers and anyone who could get at him. He was flogged, slapped in the face, spat upon, mauled obscenely, and debased. They blindfolded him and asked him to show them a "sign," since he was such a man of miracles and wonders. They put a purple robe on him like a theatrical king and made a ringlet of thorns and put it on his head like a crown; and there was a mock worship of him as a ridiculous king in which the soldiers and the mob bowed and curtsied before him and made vulgar signs at him.

Meantime, when Judas saw that Jesus was condemned, he repented in horror. Had he thought Jesus would escape or miraculously save himself? Judas went to the chief priests and elders and told them that he had "betrayed the innocent blood" and wanted to return the money. The men told Judas that they were not concerned with his problems. In an agony of guilt and self-hatred, Judas flung down the thirty pieces of silver before the priests and "went and hanged himself." The priests called the money "blood money" and would not have it, but used it to buy a potter's field "to bury strangers in." (Matt. 27:3–10. But Acts 1:16–19 tells a different story of the way Judas died—by falling headlong, on land he had bought with the money, he "burst asunder.")

Now they led Jesus away toward a hill where people were commonly nailed to crosses for murder or theft—it was a place for the crucifixion of criminals. It was a place so cursed and haunted by brutal deaths that it had been named "The Place of Skulls" (Golgotha). Jesus had been so weakened by the beatings they had given him that he could not manage to carry the cross-beam of his cross very far; he stumbled. The soldiers grabbed a man who was passing by, named Simon of Cyrene, and made him carry the cross.

A little band of the curious followed. Women watched and stood apart. From a distance they kept their eyes on this ugly thing that was happening. The Twelve were nowhere to be found. They were obviously hiding, heartbroken and afraid. Where were the thousands who had so recently thronged about Jesus to the point of crushing him under? Where were the thousands who waved and strew green branches and shouted Hosannahs to him when he came into the city, on the back of a colt only several days ago? A few short days before they had acclaimed him and were willing to accept him on their own terms. Surely here was the descendant of their ancient line of kings, an ally against the collaborating priests, a rallying point for their hatred against the Rome that occupied and governed their country. When they had discovered that he had no plan that would work to their personal material advantage, that there was to be no vengeance on the foreigners they hated and the upper-class collaborators whom they loathed, they turned away from him and against him. He was no leader for them, then. When he instead called for love, forgiveness, reconciliation, from those who followed him, they left him. Yet Jesus had come to Jerusalem knowing that this very thing would happen to him.

When Jesus saw a crowd of weeping women following him he said to them, "Daughters of Jerusalem, do not weep for me but weep for yourselves and for your children." And then the tragic procession arrived at the hill called Golgotha.

It was the "third hour" (nine o'clock), and they straightaway stripped Jesus and nailed his hands to the horizontal cross-beam that Simon the Cyrene had carried. They then hoisted it up and attached it to the upright beam that was standing. They nailed his crossed feet to this beam. He suffered. They wrote in Greek, Hebrew, and Latin a sign that read THE KING OF THE JEWS and nailed it over his head. There were two men, thieves, on either side of him. In their misery they behaved in a violent way. One in his bitterness told Jesus that if he was such a savior as they had proclaimed him to be, why didn't he miraculously get them all off the damned trees of their agony? The other had a peculiar feeling that the man on the middle cross was an innocent man, and spoke to him and said, "Lord, remember me when thou comest into thy kingdom." (Luke 23:42)

All around him under the cross a little vulgar play went on. Soldiers wagged their tongues at him, whispered and shouted foul language, dared him to save himself—had he not so grandly said only yesterday that he would tear down and rebuild the Temple of Jerusalem in three days with his own hands? They were all there, getting their vengeance. Some soldiers cast lots for his clothes.

The chief priests called up to him and commented to each other that he had saved so many others yet he could not save himself. Did he remember the leaping lame, the deaf ears opened, the blind eyes suddenly seeing men "that walked like trees," those made clean and those made sane and calm—all that beloved company of men and women of faith made whole and sound.

At a distance, below the hill, aghast and beyond grief, were some of the women who had been his faithful followers and helpers, including Mary Magdalene, who had never left his side since the day he changed her life, his mother Mary, and, Mark says, "many other women which came up with him unto Jerusalem." Jesus' beloved friend John the apostle might have been there too, for we read in the Gospel of St. John that Jesus spoke down from the cross to him and asked him to take care of his mother Mary as though he were her son. (John 19:26–27)

It is written that when the "sixth hour" came (this would be noon), darkness fell over the whole land until the "ninth hour." At the "ninth hour" his agony was profound, and after uttering a great cry, he died.

A man named Joseph of Arimathea, a secret follower of Jesus—it is said that he was a member of the Sanhedrin—went to Pilate and asked him if he could take down the body of the dead man and bury him in a tomb that he had just built. Pilate was surprised that the man had died so quickly—it generally took longer; and he gave Joseph of Arimathea the body of Jesus.

When the body was wrapped in good linen it was laid in the new tomb belonging to Joseph, and a great stone was laid in front of the opening of the tomb to seal it from thieves, since it was very possible that the body might be stolen.

On the third day after this, Mary Magdalene and Mary, Jesus' mother, and another woman friend of Jesus', probably his aunt named Salome, came to the tomb and found the stone lifted away and the tomb open. They were sure that the body of Jesus had been stolen, but when they went inside they found that it was indeed not there. We are told in the record of the Gospels that a young man was sitting there and that he advised the women not to be afraid and said the words that have rung through the ages, the words that have caused centuries of disputation, unrest, uncertainty of faith, and the very risking or the very sacrifice of men's lives: "He is risen."

The women were afraid and ran away and did not say anything to anybody about what had happened. For it was still a very dangerous time, a time full of dread, failure and suspicion. When soldiers of the watch reported the absence of the body to the chief priests, they were given "large money" to say that Jesus' disciples had stolen the body while they, the guards, were asleep.

But to whom should the risen Jesus appear first, on the third day, but Mary Magdalene, the changed woman. When she saw him she ran to tell the others, but they would not believe her and thought the devils had come back into her.

A little later, he came among two of his apostles walking along the road by a village called Emmaus, and he walked with them as a stranger, revealing himself to them at the end. And later, he came to the Eleven, who were obviously hiding out—it was still such a time of terrorism and their lives were in danger—and scolded them for not believing those who had already seen him. The apostle Andrew doubted that it was Jesus, but Jesus gave proof by asking the apostles to "handle" him and to touch the wounds in his hands and side. And again, on the shore, in the early morning twilight, he was seen by some of the apostles who were fishing. Peter was so excited that he leapt into the water and swam ashore to him. They all ate bread and fish together, broiled over a fire that Jesus had made; and Jesus lovingly forgave the exultant Peter for having denied knowing him. ("Simon, Simon, behold, Satan hath desired to have you, that he may sift you as wheat. But I have prayed for thee, that thy faith fail not, and when thou art converted, strengthen thy brethren. And he said unto him, Lord, I am ready to go with thee, both in prison, and to death. And he said, I tell thee, Peter, the cock shall not crow this day, before that thou shalt thrice deny that thou knowest me.") (Luke 22:31–34)

When Jesus finally left these men whom Luke describes as "these men who have companied with us all the time that the Lord Jesus went in and out among us, beginning from the baptism of John unto that same day that he was taken from us" (Acts 1:21, 22), he said to them, "Go ye into all the world and preach the Gospel to every creature." He then reminded them that their work in the world was to carry on what they had all begun together and had witnessed together. Go on, was what he was saying. Go on, now, and continue what we began together, because "lo, I am with you always, even unto the end of the world."

II

Other Thirsts,
Other Hungers
Some people in Jesus' life

THERE are many unforgettable people living brief, vivid lives in the Gospels. Their encounters with Jesus as he passed along their way reflect the man himself, the quality of his mind and heart. The very nature of him comes close to us when we see him with these nameless men and women of deep instinctive belief. They and Jesus have become deathless witnesses for each other.

Some came to Jesus with ready faith; others, weaker, faltered and then suddenly surrendered themselves to him and left with abiding and authoritative faith. It was their faith that Jesus loved and that moved him to help them. Others came into his presence, running or kneeling or stealing under the darkness of night, in a desperate attempt to find something from him that might save them from emptiness, a wrong life, a lost way. They came in humility and in hard need but, in the end, they lacked the final courage to take a stand and give their belief to him openly and wholly. They are the "almost."

All make it known that they are searching—to be made "whole," to find "soundness," to be made not to thirst or to hunger again; that they want to be new, fulfilled, living, alive. Here are several of those people, indestructible and immortal figures of hope, near-hope, and hopelessness, through whom we can glimpse the living Jesus and who might be our very neighbors, or our very selves.

The Gospel records show us the *personal* nature of Jesus' message. It was and is for each man. As he walked, he talked to and helped those without "light," without "water," without "bread," with no door, no shepherd and their flock scattered or lost, no vine for the branch; sick with hate and fear; lame, deaf, blind; insensate with rage, possessed and self-divided by jealousy, lust. Where he walked and went was among the afflicted, the addicted, the outcast, the desolate, the forlorn. On the roads and in the mountains, in the streets of towns, in the houses of villagers, by the shore, he told that he had personal good news for every man. No man was unworthy of receiving that news no matter how far away from such good news he might be, since good news meant that a "kingdom" of good was possible and could be had by everybody *right now* if only they would take it. He said that we cannot live without our dignity, we cannot live without our humanity, we cannot live without our own respect for ourselves. We cannot harm these, for they are the Spirit in us and, he said, that is what I am and that is what I give you: I am the dignity in you and I will let no one harm that, or I will bring it back to you if you have lost it; come to me.

This man Jesus was a man on earth, a man of flesh as well as of spirit. He knew how flesh hurts. He touched, with his hands, *physical* humanity; he handled the flawed bodies of thousands. Jesus loved the physical world and the suffering creature in man. He was so much a part of the substance of nature that it was the very material of his teaching (a grain of wheat, a mustard seed, a fruit tree that withers, is barren, or produces bad fruit; the grass that is like flesh that the wind blows over and withers). The man of the spirit honored the flesh which, though it die, must be straightened if it is bowed over, made sound if it is unsound, made clean if it is fouled with disease, by restoring and mending. He did it with his own hands and often with his own spittle. He loved the humanity of flesh that he touched, embraced, handled. He was a great gentle Nurse, soother of flesh as well as comforter of spirit. His physical embrace of humanity was a grand enveloping caress, a lifting up in his arms of the collapsed and fallen, a flesh-and-bone support for the stumbling, a warm broad human breast for the fainting head of the weak.

His contemporaries were drawn to his dynamic and haunting, charming and mysterious *physical* presence. The physical Jesus strides in energy and power across the pages of the Gospels. He was not attacked only intellectually in catch-questions and cross-examinations by his judges and accusers. His very body was assailed, slapped, spat upon, whipped, struck with stones. The palms of his hands and the brows of his feet were driven through with nails. He "sweated blood" in the garden of Gethsemane. When his assassins ran upon him to seize him in the garden, they "went backward and fell to the ground" in amazement at the mysterious physical beauty and power that charged out of his person.

Jesus obviously loved the natural, physical world or he would not have so denounced those who corrupted it, and the beautiful things of the earth, or he would not have rebuked so sternly those who made them ugly. And he loved men and women above all as though they were his own children, his brothers and sisters, all his very own. He went away, many times, by himself to the wilderness, by rivers and on mountains, in deserts, living among the wild beasts and eating food that grew wild. He touched brute nature and was toughened by the reality of wild nature.

He thought of himself as being in nature—and he spoke of himself as a sheep, as a lamb, as a mothering hen: "O Jerusalem! Jerusalem! which killest the prophets, and stonest them that are sent unto thee; how often would I have gathered thy children together, as a hen doth gather her brood under her wings, and ye would not!" (Luke 13:34) Or as a gentle ox or beast of cartage: "Take my yoke upon you, and learn of me: for I am meek and lowly in heart: and ye shall find rest unto your souls. For my yoke is easy, and my burden is light." (Matt. 11:29–30)

1. The Other Water

ONE day Jesus came to a city in Samaria called Sychar, where the ancient Jacob's Well was. As he sat at the well resting and cooling off from his journey, a woman came to the well to draw water. Jesus said to her, "I am thirsty, give me a cool drink of water." The woman was surprised and answered smartly, "You are a Jew and I am a Samaritan. You know that Jews and Samaritans have nothing to do with each other. Why is it then that you are not only speaking to me but asking me to give you water?" Jesus answered, "If you knew who it is who asks you for water you would have asked him to give *you* a drink. He would have given you living water."

The woman became very astute. "Sir," she said, "since the well is very deep and you have nothing to draw water with, you cannot even fetch water from *this* well. Where on earth could you find that other water, that 'living water' that you speak about? Isn't this well that our ancestor Jacob gave to us worthy enough for you? Are you greater than Jacob, who drank of this very well himself, and his children and his cattle?" Jesus said, "But whoever drinks of this water will be thirsty again. Whoever drinks of that other water will never again thirst. That other water will be like a well springing up into everlasting life within him."

The woman suddenly became humble and broke through her disguise of sophistication and revealed the emptiness and the thirst of her life. "Sir," she said, quietly, "give me this other water so that I may never be thirsty again, nor have to come here and draw up this water that gives no relief."

Jesus, now having drawn the woman into her deepest living self, said, "Go find your husband and come back with him to me." The woman then confessed, "I have no husband." Jesus came back swiftly. "To be sure you have not, for although you have had five husbands the man you now live with is not your husband." The woman, as-

tounded, said, "Sir, you are a Prophet," and putting down her water pot ran into the town and
said to those she came upon, "Come see a man, who
told me everything that I have ever done! Surely
this man must be the Christ. He told me everything
that I have ever done!"

And when the people saw the glowing look in
her face, which before had been lusterless, they
knew something had changed her. They ran to find
the man because of what the woman had said about
him and because of the great new life in her. When
they found the man and spoke to him, they believed in him, too. (John 4:5–42)

2. Waiting for the Moving of the Water

BY the sheep market in Jerusalem there was a pool called Bethesda, which was surrounded by five porches. On these porches lay a great number of afflicted people, waiting. For it was said that at certain times an angel touched the pool and "troubled" the water. Whoever was able to get into the water after it had been moved would be cured of his affliction.

A paralyzed man who had suffered his infirmity for thirty-eight years lay by the pool, waiting for the moving of the water. When Jesus passed by one day and saw the man lying there, he knew that the man had been waiting there for a long, long time. He asked the man, "Why have you been here so long and are not healed?" The infirm man answered him, "Sir, I have no one to help me into the waters when they move. Each time I try, another pushes in front of me." Jesus said, "Well, then, get up and pick up your cot and walk on."

Immediately, without question, the man stood up, folded his cot and walked away.

Now this was the Sabbath and those who saw the cured man carrying his cot in the street said to him, "What are you doing carrying your cot on the Sabbath? You know it is against the law."

The man answered, "The one who made me strong again told me to take my cot and go home." The men asked him who the man was who had the authority to give him permission to carry his cot through the streets on the Sabbath Day. "I do not know who he was," the cured man said. "As soon as he told me to get up and walk, he went away into the crowds."

When Jesus heard that the cured man was in trouble, he went to look for him and found him in the Temple. He said, "Now that you are strong again, respect your strength and the faith that gave it back to you. Go on now."

The cured man then ran away, carrying his cot and calling out to the authorities that he had found the man and that his name was Jesus. (John 5:2–15)

3. The Pool of Siloam

WHEN Jesus encountered a man who was born blind, he made clay out of the ground mixed with his spittle and he put the clay on the eyes of the blind man. "Now go and wash your eyes in the pool of Siloam."

Jesus went on his way and the blind man went to the pool and washed and saw. His neighbors who found him walking around could not believe that he was the same blind man who had sat and begged, but the blind man said, "I am the same one." "Then how were your eyes opened?" they asked him. The man said, "A man that is called Jesus made clay and put it on my eyes and told me to go and wash in the pool of Siloam; and I went and washed and I saw." "Where is this man?" they asked. The seeing man said, "I don't know."

Now this was the Sabbath Day when Jesus had

opened the blind man's eyes. His neighbors took him to the Pharisees, and the Pharisees asked him how he had received his sight. The man said again, "He put clay on my eyes and I washed and now I see." "But," said some of the Pharisees, "whoever this man is, he has nothing to do with God and he must be a sinner because he has broken the law of the Sabbath." But others said, "Yet how can a man be a sinner and perform such a miracle?" The Pharisees were disturbed and were divided among themselves. They turned again to the seeing man and said, "Who do you think he was? What do you have to say about him who opened your eyes?" "I don't know," the seeing man said, "except that most certainly he must be a Prophet." Those who had not known the once blind man said they would not believe that he had been blind until his parents were called. His parents came and said, "Well, this is our son and we know that he was born blind. But by what means he now sees we do not know, nor do we know who has opened his eyes. But he is of age. Ask him. He can speak for himself." The seeing man's parents, although they were overjoyed and astonished, were afraid to show their feelings for fear they would be punished and put out of the synagogue.

The doubters said to the seeing man, "It is obvious that whoever this man is that gave you sight is a sinner since he did not keep the Sabbath. Give God the credit." The seeing man said simply, "Well, I don't know whether he is what you call a 'sinner' or not, but one thing I do know is that I was blind and now I see."

The men began to torment him. They were obsessed, and they said to him again, "What did he do to you? How did he open your eyes?" The man said, "I told you several times but you don't seem to listen to me. Why do you want me to tell you again? Could it be that you might want to be his disciples?" This angered the men and they snapped at him, "You might be his disciple, but we are Moses' disciples. We know that God spoke to Moses. As for this fellow, we don't know who he is or where he came from."

Now the seeing man said, "Why here is a marvelous thing. That you can go on disputing and disclaiming what happened to *me!* All I know is that I see! And I'll tell you something more," he went on, suddenly finding spiritual insight. "If this man who put clay on my eyes were not from God then he could not have done what he did."

This enraged the doubters and they said to him, "*You* who were born full of imperfection, are trying to teach *us?*" And they threw him out of the synagogue.

Jesus had word that the once blind man had been cast out, and when he found him he said to him, "Tell me, do you believe in the Son of God?" The seeing man answered and said, "Tell me, sir, but who is he so that I can show him my faith?"

Jesus said to him, "You have not only seen him but you are talking with him."

And the seeing man said, "Lord, I believe"; and showed him all his love. (John 9:10–39)

4. Almost

ANOTHER time, when Jesus found his disciples surrounded by an unsettled crowd, he asked what the matter was. A man stepped out of the crowd and said, "Master, I have brought my son to you. He is possessed with a violent spirit. He tears at himself and foams at the mouth and gnashes his teeth and pines away. While you were away I asked your disciples to help my son and they could not."

Jesus was impatient with his disciples, who had not been able to help the youth, and he criticized them for their lack of faith. "Bring the child to me," he said.

When they brought the young man, he immediately fell into a fit and wallowed on the ground, foaming. "How long has he been like this?" Jesus asked the man, and the man answered, "Since he was a child. And often this madness has cast him into the fire and into water to destroy him. If you can do anything, have compassion on us and help us."

Jesus said to him, "If you can have faith, all things are possible." The father of the young man cried out, "Lord, I do believe—almost! Help me in my unbelief!"

At this, Jesus said to the spirit in the young man, "Come out of him and enter him no more." The spirit cried out and tore through the young man and came out of him; and he lay as if he were dead.

"He is dead," those who were around him said.

But Jesus took the young man by the hand and lifted him up; and he stood up and was at peace. (Mark 9:17–27)

5. The Young Man Who Came Running

As Jesus was walking along a road one day there was the usual excitement all around him and a throng of people following him. Suddenly out of the throng a young man came running and knelt before Jesus in high emotion. "Good Master," he said, "I know of all your wonderful works and what you have done for people. Please tell me what I must do to find the joy and fullness of life that I do not have?"

Jesus said to the young man, observing that he was overwrought, and trying to calm him, "If you know me, then you know the Commandments: Do not commit adultery; Do not kill; Do not steal; Do not bear false witness; Do not defraud; Honor thy father and mother."

"Master," the young man said, "I have observed all these commandments all of my life. And still," he cried out, "I cannot find my way. There is something lacking."

Jesus suddenly looked intently upon the young man and felt great love and compassion for him. For he recognized that something profound was missing in this young man. He was a very rich young man, who obviously had everything he could want, money, comfort, love, beauty; yet he was restless and empty.

Jesus said to him, "You have all these things and yet one thing you lack. You like your things more than anything else in the world, even more than yourself. If you will sell all you have and give up all your riches to the poor and come and follow me you will find what you are so desperately searching for. Can you give up what you seem most to care about, yet which is the very cause of your despair? Can you do that?"

The young man fell back at this request and looked up at Jesus with a look that showed his anguish. He was still afraid; he could not give up. Almost ready, at the very edge of total giving of himself, the desperate young man turned and ran away in the dust of the road. (Mark 10:17–22)

6. The Crumbs That Fall from the Master's Table

WHEN Jesus was on the coasts of Tyre and Sidon he met a woman of that territory. The woman was Greek, a Gentile, and it was the custom for Jews not to speak to Gentiles and certainly not to Gentile women. But the woman cried out to Jesus, "Have mercy on me, for my daughter is grievously possessed with an illness of the mind."

Jesus did not answer her, although his disciples came and begged him to send her away because she had been crying after them. It was then that Jesus said to the woman, "I am only sent to those of Israel." But the woman had great faith in him and said, "Lord, help me!"

"But I cannot take the bread that is meant for the children and cast it to the dogs of the house," Jesus declared. The woman said, "I know that is true, Lord, yet the dogs eat of the crumbs that fall from their master's tables."

Jesus was so astonished at the woman's great belief in him, although he had been very strict with her, testing her, that he praised her and said, "O, woman, great is thy faith. It will be as you ask it." And her daughter was made whole from that very hour. (Matt. 15:21–28)

7. The Other Bread

AFTER Jesus had fed the multitude of some five thousand with five loaves of bread and two fish, the throngs were so near riot with excitement that Jesus had to escape for the sake of his own safety. The next day the milling thousands found him and thronged to him. Jesus became very severe with them and spoke to them about the two kinds of bread.

"You are not seeking me but the bread that I can give you to eat, as of yesterday. But don't labor for food that gives only passing ease to your hunger. Strive only for that other food, that other bread that leaves men never hungry again." He spoke of the "bread of God" that a man might eat "and not die"; the "true bread" that gives life to the world. "He who comes to me will never be hungry," he told them. "I am the bread of life."

"Sir," they said, "give us that bread."

But many of Jesus' followers could not accept the kind of imagery that pictured Jesus as bread that he would give to men "to eat of" in order to live forever. They "strove among themselves," saying, "How can this man give us his flesh to eat?" Many "went back and walked no more with him." Jesus upbraided those who turned away from him and said that they did not understand what he was saying because they did not believe. "Isn't it clear to you that I speak of the spirit that gives life?" he asked. "What the flesh offers does not last. *That* is the kind of hunger and thirst I speak of." Then he turned to his twelve apostles and asked them if they were going to turn away from him, too, as the others had. Peter answered, "Lord, to whom shall we go? Thou hast the words of eternal life, and we believe. . . ."

8. The Man Who Came by Night

A man of power, a leading Pharisee and a member of the Sanhedrin, a man named Nicodemus, couldn't get Jesus out of his mind. He kept thinking about the things he said and his mind was filled with questions. As a member of the high council that was, indeed, trying to find ways to entrap and to kill Jesus, how could he, Nicodemus, be caught talking with him?

But he suddenly knew that he had to see this man face to face. He waited until it was dark and went, by night, to Jesus. They talked. Nicodemus said, "Sir, we know that you are a teacher sent here by God, for only a man who is of God could do these mighty things which we have all seen." Jesus observed the man quietly and then said, "In order to see the Kingdom of God, a man has to be born again. There are two kingdoms, one of the flesh and which can be seen and heard, the other of the spirit, in which you have to have faith and believe in."

Nicodemus looked bewildered by this statement, but his eyes were searching Jesus' eyes in the dark for a clearer meaning of what he was saying. "Don't be confused by my saying that you must be born again. The wind blows where it wants to, and although we can hear it we cannot tell where it comes from or where it is going; and the same is true for those who are born of the spirit." Nicodemus was still confused and he asked how such things could be, that a man who is born once could be born twice, could go back into his mother's womb and be born again. Jesus became firm now and said, "You, who are one of the leaders of Israel, can't comprehend what I am saying? I speak of the things we know and see, and yet you don't believe me. How on earth, then, can you believe if I speak to you of things that cannot be heard or seen but must be believed in, by faith?" Nicodemus waited to hear more. His hunger for answers, his thirst for belief were obvious to Jesus.

"God did not send his son into the world to condemn it but to save it. No one who believes in him will be lost, but whoever refuses to believe is the one who is lost." There was silence. Then Jesus spoke quietly and gravely to the very center of the man who had so needed the truth that he had risked his life, perhaps, to come in the dark to a notorious enemy. "It is those who refuse to believe, who prefer darkness to the light, because they are afraid and unhappy and therefore feel evil within them. Anybody who does wrong hates the light and avoids it for fear he will be found out. But the man who lives by the truth and who believes, comes out into the light and lets himself be plainly seen."

We are told no more. Surely Nicodemus got up and walked away into the night out of which he came. We do not know what bitterness followed him away or what inner light shone in on him, as he walked off, that changed him, secretly, forever after that meeting. But we do know that later, when the officers had failed to follow their orders to catch Jesus and bring him to the Pharisees, the high officials, among whom was Nicodemus, were angry ("Why haven't you brought him?" The officers answered, "Never man spake like this man."), and they wondered if the officers were also now deceived by this man. "Have any of our rulers or Pharisees believed on him?" they asked. "Such people as this Jesus, who do not know the Law, are cursed!"

Nicodemus, sitting among them, asked quietly, "But does our Law, that you speak of, judge a man before it has heard him out and before it knows what the man has done?"

The Pharisees shot glances at Nicodemus and snarled, "Are you, too, from Galilee?"

After Jesus had died, Nicodemus came to help Joseph of Arimathea prepare the body for burial, and he brought expensive and precious spices for the embalmment. And he helped Joseph wrap Jesus' body in linen and put him in the tomb. (John 3:1-21; John 19:39-40)

III

Words of Jesus

The quality of his mind and
his way of talking to people

I am the door: by me if any man enter in,
he shall be saved, and shall go in and out,
and find pasture.

(John 10:9)

I am the good shepherd: the good shepherd
giveth his life for the sheep.

(John 10:11)

I am come a light into the world, that
whosoever believeth on me should not
abide in darkness.

(John 12:46)

I am the vine, ye are the branches. He that
abideth in me, and I in him, the same
bringeth forth much fruit; for without me
ye can do nothing.

(John 15:5)

Verily, verily, I say unto you, Except a
corn of wheat fall into the ground and die,
it abideth alone: but if it die, it bringeth
forth much fruit.

(John 12:24)

Hearken: Behold, there went out a sower
to sow:

And it came to pass, as he sowed, some
fell by the wayside, and the fowls of the air
came and devoured it up.

And some fell on stony ground, where it
had not much earth; and immediately it
sprang up, because it had no depth of earth:

But when the sun was up, it was
scorched; and because it had no root, it
withered away.

And some fell among thorns, and the
thorns grew up, and choked it, and it
yielded no fruit.

And another fell on good ground, and
did yield fruit that sprang up and increased,

and brought forth, some thirty, and some sixty, and some a hundred.

And he said unto them, He that hath ears to hear, let him hear.

And when he was alone, they that were about him with the twelve, asked of him the parable.

And he said unto them, Unto you it is given to know the mystery of the kingdom of God: but unto them that are without, all these things are done in parables:

That seeing they may see, and not perceive; and hearing they may hear, and not understand; lest at any time they should be converted, and their sins should be forgiven them.

And he said unto them, Know ye not this parable? and how then will ye know all parables?

The sower soweth the word.

And these are they by the wayside, where the word is sown; but when they have heard, Satan cometh immediately, and taketh away the word that was sown in their hearts.

And these are they likewise which are sown on stony ground; who, when they have heard the word, immediately receive it with gladness;

And have no root in themselves, and so endure but for a time; afterward, when affliction or persecution ariseth for the word's sake, immediately they are offended.

And these are they which are sown among thorns; such as hear the word.

And the cares of this world, and the deceitfulness of riches, and the lusts of other things entering in, choke the word, and it becometh unfruitful.

And these are they which are sown on good ground; such as hear the word, and receive it, and bring forth fruit, some thirty-fold, some sixty, and some a hundred.

And he said unto them, Is a candle

brought to be put under a bushel, or under a bed? and not to be set on a candlestick?

For there is nothing hid, which shall not be manifested; neither was anything kept secret, but that it should come abroad.

If any man have ears to hear, let him hear.

And he said unto them, Take heed what ye hear. With what measure ye mete, it shall be measured to you; and unto you that hear shall more be given.

For he that hath, to him shall be given; and he that hath not, from him shall be taken even that which he hath.

And he said, So is the kingdom of God, as if a man should cast seed into the ground;

And should sleep, and rise night and day, and the seed should spring and grow up, he knoweth not how.

For the earth bringeth forth fruit of herself; first the blade, then the ear, after that the full corn in the ear.

But when the fruit is brought forth, immediately he putteth in the sickle, because the harvest is come.

And he said, Whereunto shall we liken the kingdom of God? or with what comparison shall we compare it?

It is like a grain of mustard seed, which, when it is sown in the earth, is less than all the seeds that be in the earth;

But when it is sown, it groweth up, and becometh greater than all herbs, and shooteth out great branches; so that the fowls of the air may lodge under the shadow of it.

(Mark 4:3–32)

The kingdom of heaven is likened unto a man which sowed good seed in his field:

But while men slept, his enemy came and sowed tares among the wheat, and went his way.

But when the blade was sprung up, and brought forth fruit, then appeared the tares also.

So the servants of the householder came

and said unto him, Sir, didst not thou sow good seed in thy field? from whence then hath it tares?

He said unto them, An enemy hath done this. The servants said unto him, Wilt thou then that we go and gather them up?

But he said, Nay; lest while ye gather up the tares, ye root up also the wheat with them.

Let both grow together until the harvest: and in the time of harvest I will say to the reapers, Gather ye together first the tares, and bind them in bundles to burn them: but gather the wheat into my barn.

(*Matt. 13:24–30*)

How think ye? if a man have a hundred sheep, and one of them be gone astray, doth he not leave the ninety and nine, and goeth into the mountains, and seeketh that which is gone astray?

And if so be that he find it, verily I say unto you, he rejoiceth more of that sheep,

than of the ninety and nine which went
not astray.

Even so it is not the will of your Father
which is in heaven, that one of these little
ones should perish.

(Matt. 18:12–14)

A certain man had a fig tree planted in his
vineyard; and he came and sought fruit
thereon, and found none.

Then he said unto the dresser of his
vineyard, Behold, these three years I come
seeking fruit on this fig tree, and find none:
cut it down; why cumbereth it the ground?

And he answering said unto him, Lord,
let it alone this year also, till I shall dig
about it, and dung it:

And if it bear fruit, well: and if not, then
after that thou shall cut it down.

(Luke 13:6–9)

I am come to send fire on the earth; and
what will I, if it be already kindled?

But I have a baptism to be baptized with; and how am I straitened till it be accomplished!

Suppose ye that I am come to give peace on earth? I tell you, Nay; but rather division:

For from henceforth there shall be five in one house divided, three against two, and two against three.

The father shall be divided against the son, and the son against the father; the mother against the daughter, and the daughter against the mother; the mother-in-law against her daughter-in-law, and the daughter-in-law against her mother-in-law.

(*Luke 12:49–53*)

Think not that I am come to send peace on earth: I came not to send peace, but a sword.

For I am come to set a man at variance

against his father, and the daughter against her mother, and the daughter-in-law against her mother-in-law.

And a man's foes shall be they of his own household.

(Matt. 10:34–36)

And he said, A certain man had two sons;

And the younger of them said to his father, Father, give me the portion of goods that falleth to me, And he divideth unto them his living. . . .

And when he had spent all, there arose a mighty famine in that land; and he began to be in want.

And he went and joined himself to a citizen of that country; and he sent him into his fields to feed swine.

And he would fain have filled his belly with the husks that the swine did eat: and no man gave unto him.

And when he came to himself, he said,

How many hired servants of my father's have bread enough and to spare, and I perish with hunger!

I will arise and go to my father, and will say unto him, Father, I have sinned against heaven, and before thee,

And am no more worthy to be called thy son: make me as one of thy hired servants.

And he rose, and came to his father. But when he was yet a great way off, his father saw him, and had compassion, and ran, and fell on his neck, and kissed him.

And the son said unto him, Father, I have sinned against heaven, and in thy sight, and am no more worthy to be called thy son.

But the father said to his servants, Bring forth the best robe, and put it on him; and put a ring on his hand, and shoes on his feet:

And bring hither the fatted calf, and kill it; and let us eat and be merry;

For this my son was dead, and is alive again; he was lost, and is found. And they began to be merry.

Now his elder son was in the field; and as he came and drew nigh to the house, he heard music and dancing.

And he called one of the servants, and asked what these things meant.

And he said unto him, Thy brother is come; and thy father hath killed the fatted calf, because he hath received him safe and sound.

And he was angry, and would not go in: therefore came his father out, and entreated him.

And he answering said to his father, Lo, these many years do I serve thee, neither transgressed I at any time thy commandment; and yet thou never gavest me a kid, that I might make merry with my friends:

But as soon as this thy son was come, which hath devoured thy living with harlots, thou hast killed for him the fatted calf.

And he said unto him, Son, thou art ever

with me, and all that I have is thine.

It was meet that we should make merry, and be glad: for this thy brother was dead, and is alive again; and was lost, and is found.

(Luke 15:11–32)

And he said also unto his disciples, There was a certain rich man, which had a steward; and the same was accused unto him that he had wasted his goods.

And he called him, and said unto him, How is it that I hear this of thee? give an account of thy stewardship; for thou mayest be no longer steward.

Then the steward said within himself, What shall I do? for my lord taketh away from me the stewardship: I cannot dig; to beg I am ashamed.

I am resolved what to do, that, when I am put out of the stewardship, they may receive me into their houses.

So he called every one of his lord's debtors unto him, and said unto the first, how much owest thou unto my lord?

And he said, A hundred measures of oil. And he said unto him, Take thy bill and sit down quickly, and write fifty.

Then said he to another, And how much owest thou? And he said, A hundred measures of wheat. And he said unto him, Take thy bill, and write fourscore.

And the lord commended the unjust steward, because he had done wisely; for the children of this world are in their generation wiser than the children of light.

And I say unto you, Make to yourselves friends of the mammon of unrighteousness; that, when ye fail, they may receive you into everlasting habitations.

(Luke 16:1–9)

And the Lord said, Who then is that faithful and wise steward, whom his lord shall make ruler over his household, to give them their portion of meat in due season?

Blessed is that servant, whom his lord

when he cometh shall find so doing.

Of a truth I say unto you, that he will make him ruler over all that he hath.

But and if that servant say in his heart, My lord delayeth his coming; and shall begin to beat the menservants and maidens, and to eat and drink, and to be drunken;

The lord of that servant will come in a day when he looketh not for him, and at an hour when he is not aware, and will cut him in sunder, and will appoint him his portion with the unbelievers.

And that servant, which knew his lord's will, and prepared not himself, neither did according to his will, shall be beaten with many stripes.

But he that knew not, and did commit things worthy of stripes, shall be beaten with few stripes. For unto whomsoever much is given, of him shall be much required; and to whom men have committed much, of him they will ask more.

(Luke 12:42–48)

And he said unto them, which of you shall have a friend, and shall go unto him at midnight, and say unto him, Friend, lend me three loaves;

For a friend of mine in his journey is come to me, and I have nothing to set before him?

And he from within shall answer and say, Trouble me not: the door is now shut, and my children are with me in bed; I cannot rise and give thee.

I say unto you, Though he will not rise and give him, because he is his friend, yet because of his importunity he will rise and give him as many as he needeth.

And I say unto you, Ask, and it shall be

given you; seek, and ye shall find; knock, and it shall be opened unto you.

For every one that asketh receiveth; and he that seeketh findeth; and to him that knocketh it shall be opened.

If a son shall ask bread of any of you that is a father, will he give him a stone? or if he ask a fish, will he for a fish give him a serpent?

Or if he shall ask an egg, will he offer him a scorpion?

If ye then, bring evil, know how to give good gifts unto your children; how much more shall your heavenly Father give the Holy Spirit to them that ask him?

(Luke 11:5–13)

But whereunto shall I liken this generation? It is like unto children sitting in the markets, and calling unto their fellows,

And saying, We have piped unto you,

and ye have not danced; we have mourned
unto you, and ye have not lamented.

For John came neither eating nor
drinking, and they say, He hath a devil.

The Son of man came eating and
drinking, and they say, Behold a man
gluttonous, and a winebibber, a friend of
publicans and sinners. But wisdom is
justified of her children.

(*Matt. 11:16–19*)

Come unto me, all ye that labor and are
heavy laden, and I will give you rest.

Take my yoke upon you, and learn of
me; for I am meek and lowly in heart: and
ye shall find rest unto your souls.

For my yoke is easy, and my burden is
light.

(*Matt. 11:28–30*)

The same day there came certain of the
Pharisees, saying unto him, Get thee out,

and depart hence: for Herod will kill thee.

And he said unto them, Go ye, and tell that fox, Behold, I cast out devils, and I do cures today and tomorrow, and the third day I shall be perfected.

Nevertheless I must walk today, and tomorrow, and the day following: for it cannot be that a prophet perish out of Jerusalem.

(Luke 13:31–33)

Salt is good: but if the salt have lost his savour, wherewith shall it be seasoned?
(Luke 14:34)

He that loveth his life shall lose it; and he that hateth his life in this world shall keep it unto life eternal.

If any man serve me, let him follow me; and where I am, there shall also my servant be: if any man serve me, him will my Father honor.

(John 12:25–26)

A new commandment I give unto you,
That ye love one another; as I have loved
you, that ye also love one another.

By this shall all men know that ye are my
disciples, if ye have love one to another.

(John 13:34–35)

Ask, and it shall be given you; seek, and ye
shall find; knock, and it shall be opened
unto you:

For every one that asketh receiveth; and
he that seeketh findeth; and to him that
knocketh it shall be opened.

Or what man is there of you, whom if
his son ask bread, will he give him a stone?

Or if he ask a fish, will he give him a
serpent?

If ye then, being evil, know how to give good gifts unto your children, how much more shall your Father which is in heaven give good things to them that ask him?

Therefore all things whatsoever ye would that men should do to you, do ye even so to them: for this is the law and the prophets.

(Matt. 7:7–12)

Wherefore I say unto thee, Her sins, which are many, are forgiven; for she loved much: but to whom little is forgiven, the same loveth little.

(Luke 7:47)

Did ye never read in the scriptures, The stone which the builders rejected, the same is become the head of the corner: this is the Lord's doing, and it is marvelous in our eyes?

Therefore say I unto you, The kingdom of God shall be taken from you, and given to a nation bringing forth the fruits thereof.

And whosoever shall fall on this stone shall be broken: but on whomsoever it shall fall, it will grind him to powder.

(Matt. 21:42–44)

The light of the body is the eye: if therefore thine eye be single, thy whole body shall be full of light.

But if thine eye be evil, thy whole body shall be full of darkness. If therefore the light that is in thee be darkness, how great is that darkness!

No man can serve two masters: for either he will hate the one, and love the other; or else he will hold to the one and despise the other. Ye cannot serve God and mammon.

Therefore I say unto you, Take no thought for your life, what ye shall eat, or what ye shall drink; nor yet for your body, what ye shall put on. Is not the life more than meat, and the body than raiment?

Behold the fowls of the air: for they sow not, neither do they reap, nor gather into barns; yet your heavenly Father feedeth them. Are ye not much better than they?

Which of you by taking thought can add one cubit unto his stature?

And why take ye thought for raiment? Consider the lilies of the field, how they grow; they toil not, neither do they spin:

And yet I say unto you, That even Solomon in all his glory was not arrayed like one of these.

Wherefore, if God so clothe the grass of the field, which today is, and tomorrow is cast into the oven, shall he not much more clothe you, O ye of little faith?

Therefore take no thought, saying, What shall we eat? or, What shall we drink? or, Wherewithal shall we be clothed?

(For after all these things do the Gentiles seek:) for your heavenly Father knoweth that ye have need of all these things.

But seek ye first the kingdom of God, and his righteousness; and all these things shall be added unto you.

Take therefore no thought for the morrow: for the morrow shall take thought for the things of itself. Sufficient unto the day is the evil thereof.

(*Matt. 6:22–34*)